THE NATURE KIDS GUIDE TO
RHINOS

DAVID ANDERSON

LP Media Inc. Publishing
Text copyright © 2026 by LP Media Inc.

For information address LP Media Inc. Publishing,
30012 Variolite St NW, Princeton MN 55371
www.lpmedia.org

Publication Data

Rhinos
The Nature Kid's Guide to Rhinos — First edition.

Summary: "Learn all about Rhinos, the Nature Kid Way"
— Provided by publisher.

ISBN: 979-8-89818-118-5

[1. Rhinos – Non-Fiction] I. Title.

Title: The Nature Kid's Guide to Rhinos

CONTENTS

Grassy Giants 4

Roaming Range 6

Super Sized 8

Horns Up 10

Sniff Strong 12

Tough Tank 14

Greens Galore 16

Rhino Rumbles 18

Rare Rivals 20

Charge 22

Run Rhino 24

Mud Baths 26

Crash Course 28

Finding Love 30

Cute Calves 32

Mighty Moms 34

Horn Hunters 36

Rescue Rangers 38

GRASSY GIANTS

White rhinos are not actually white. The name comes from a Dutch word meaning wide. This describes their flat, square lips for munching grass.

Snort! A white rhino lifts its wide head. Its big ears turn to listen.

Rhinos are huge animals. They live in Africa and Asia. These amazing giants can be found in many different places.

Rhinos make their homes in grasslands and thick bushes. Some rhinos live in tall grass and swamps. Others hide in thick rainforests and dense jungle areas. All these places have lots of plants to eat.

All rhinos need water nearby. They drink every day when they can find it. Water helps keep these big animals healthy and strong.

ROAMING RANGE

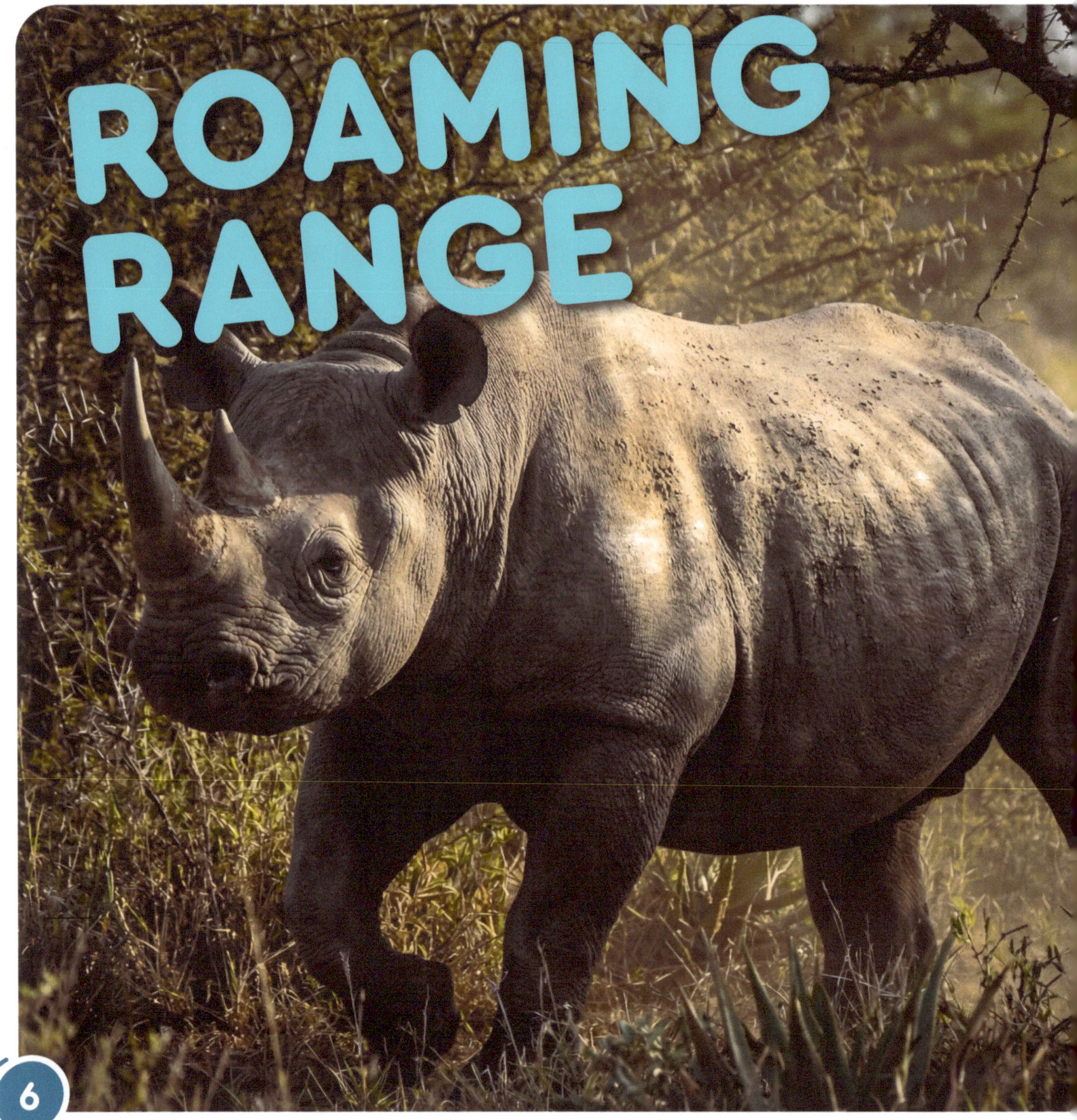

Thump! A black rhino walks through tall bushes. This is her home.

Rhinos live in areas called their "home ranges". They usually stay within their own space and know it well.

Rhinos can have very different sized home ranges. Some may use up to eight square miles. Others use much smaller areas.

Most rhinos stay close to water sources. They like areas with rivers, swamps, or watering holes nearby.

Rhinos make paths through their territory. They use the same trails over and over.

SUPER SIZED

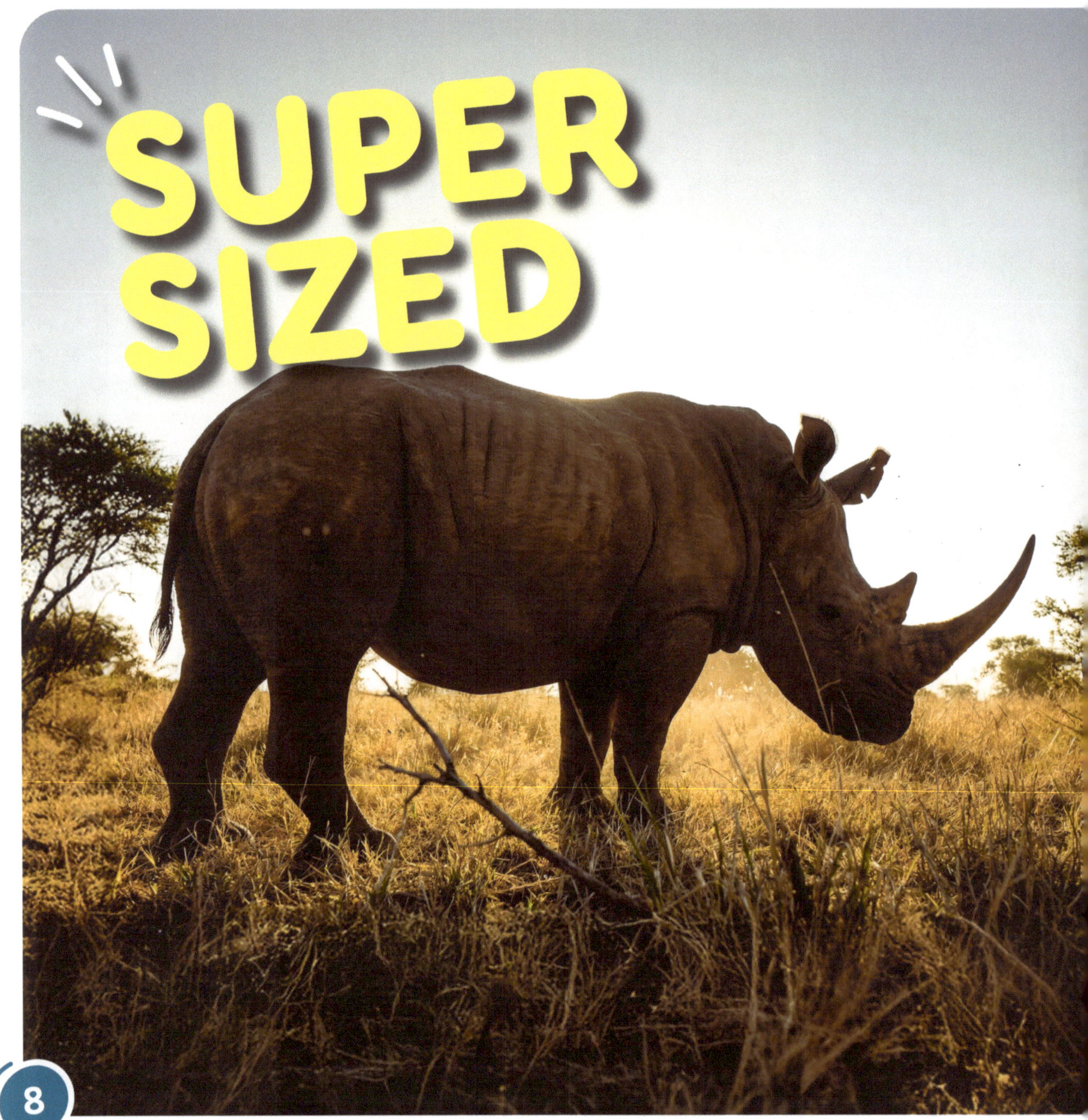

Stomp! A rhino stands in the grass. Its huge feet flatten the ground.

Rhinos are one of the biggest land animals. Only elephants are larger. These giant creatures are truly massive.

Rhinos can weigh thousands of pounds. The biggest rhinos weigh over 5,000 pounds. That is as heavy as a small truck.

Their giant heads alone can weigh hundreds of pounds. Even baby rhinos are born big, weighing around 100 pounds at birth.

White rhinos can grow over 13 feet long from nose to tail. They can run 30 miles per hour!

HORNS UP

Rhinos use their horns to dig in the ground and find water during dry times.

Crunch! A rhino rubs its horn on a rough tree trunk.

Rhino horns are not made of bone like you might think. They are made of **keratin.** This is the same stuff in your fingernails!

Rhinos can have one or two horns on their nose. The front horn is usually longer than the back horn. Some rhinos can grow horns over three feet long!

Rhino horns are very useful tools. Rhinos use their horns to dig in dirt. They also use them to move branches and protect themselves.

If a rhino's horn breaks off, it will slowly grow back over time.

SNIFF
STRONG

Sniff! A rhino lifts its nose high. It smells something far away.

Rhinos cannot see well. Their small eyes sit on the sides of their head. They can only see things clearly up close.

But rhinos have amazing noses. They can smell other animals from far away. This helps them find food and water.

Rhinos also have great hearing. Their ears turn to hear sounds all around.

A rhino can smell a human from almost half a mile away.

14

Rumble! A rhino charges at a hyena. Its thick body is like armor.

Rhinos have very thick skin. It can be almost two inches thick in some spots. This tough skin protects them from bites and scratches.

Their big bodies help keep them safe too. Most animals stay away from something so large and strong.

Rhinos also use their horns to fight. They can swing their heads fast. A rhino horn can be deadly to any attacking animal.

The Indian rhino has skin folds that look like armor plates, helping it bend.

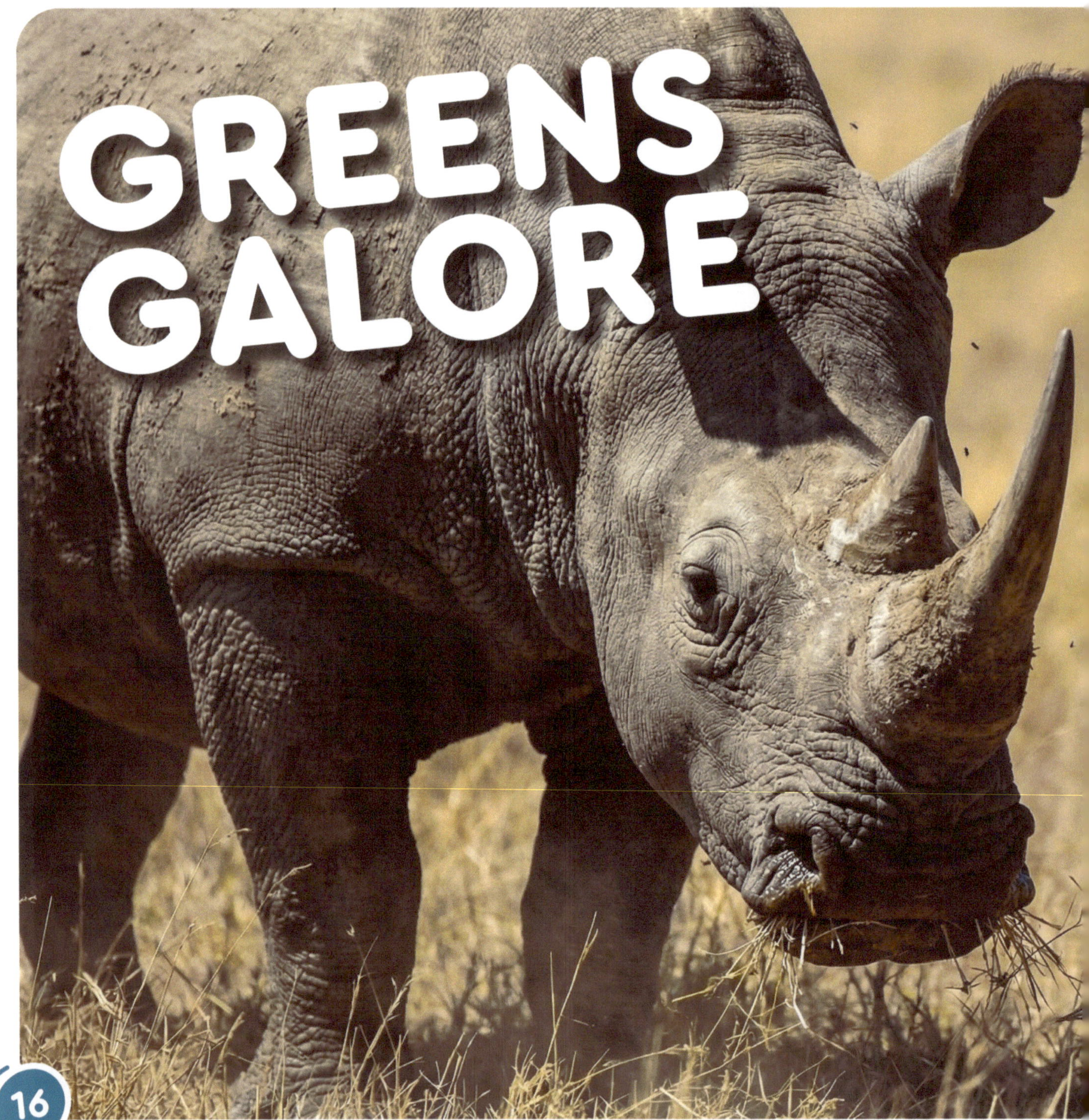

GREENS
GALORE

Chomp! A rhino bites off a big mouthful of grass. Time for lunch!

Rhinos are **herbivores**. This means they only eat plants, never meat.

Rhinos eat grass, leaves, and twigs. Their lips help them grab food easily. They spend many hours eating each day.

Rhinos also eat fruit and bark. Some rhinos love water plants.

Rhinos need lots of plants to stay healthy. They are always looking for fresh green food to munch on.

A rhino can eat up to 120 pounds of food daily.

RHINO RUMBLES

Rhinos can make sounds too low for humans to hear. These are called infrasounds.

Snort! A rhino blows air through its nose.

Rhinos make many sounds. They snort, grunt, and squeak. Each sound means something different. A loud snort can be a warning.

Mothers and babies talk to each other. Calves make high squeaking sounds. Mothers answer with soft grunts. These sounds help them stay close.

Rhinos also use smell to communicate. They leave scent marks with their dung. Other rhinos can read these smells. The scent tells them who was there. It also shows how long ago they passed by.

RARE RIVALS

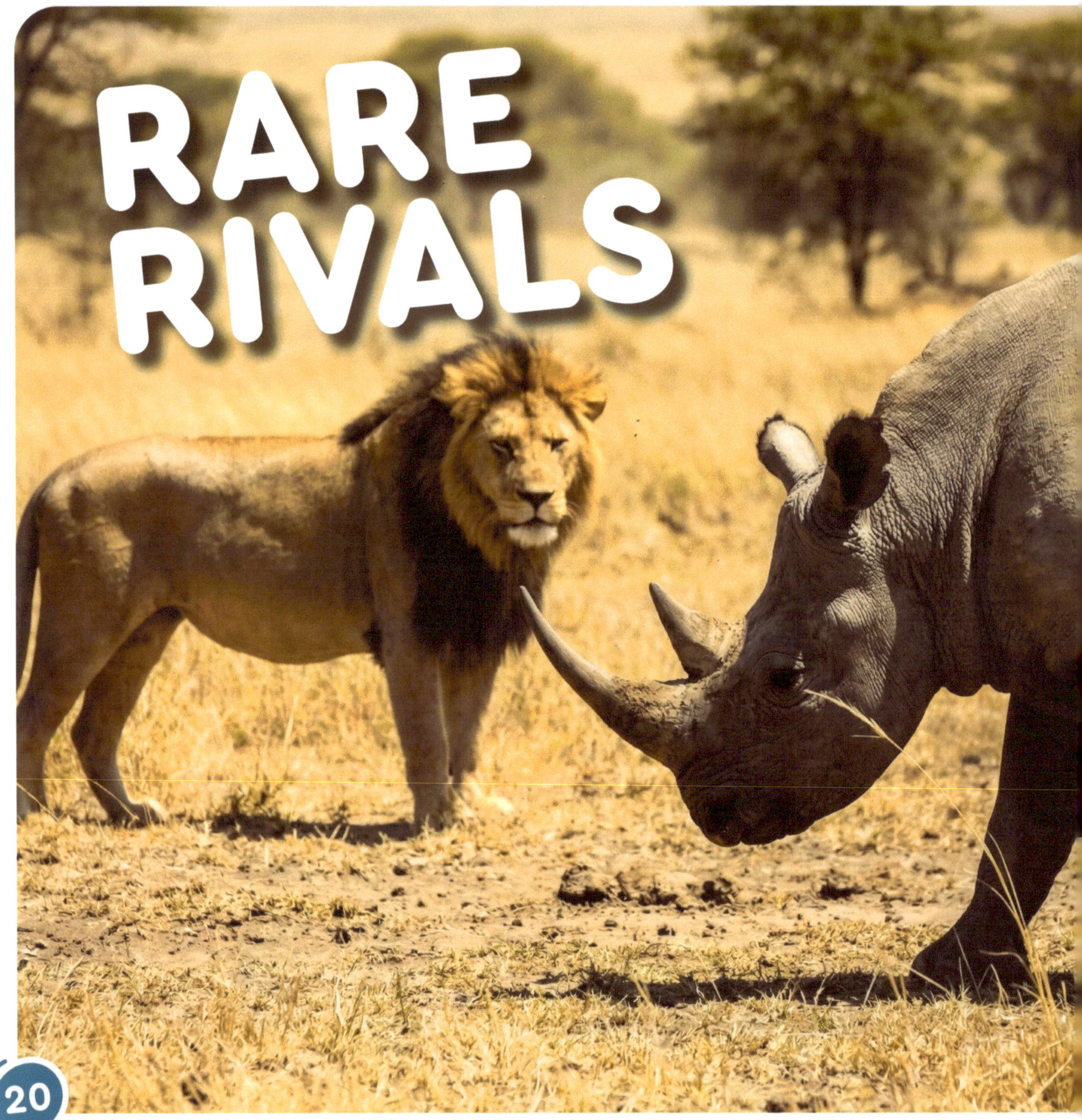

Growl! A black rhino faces a lion. Both animals stand very still.

Rhinos do not have many natural enemies. They are too big and strong for most predators.

Still, lions and hyenas sometimes hunt baby rhinos. But mother rhinos fight hard to protect their calves. A charging rhino scares most predators away.

Crocodiles can also be dangerous near water. They may try to grab a young rhino drinking at a river. Adult rhinos are usually too large to attack.

In Asia, tigers have also been known to attack young rhinos near water holes.

CHARGE

Whoosh! A rhino spins around fast. Dust flies everywhere!

Rhinos charge when they feel scared. They can turn quickly despite their size. A charging rhino is very fast and powerful.

Rhinos often charge at things they cannot see clearly. Their eyesight is poor. They may run toward sounds or smells instead.

Many rhino charges are warnings. The rhino often stops before hitting. This scares enemies away.

A mother rhino will charge at any animal that comes near her baby, even elephants!

24

Swoosh! A rhino runs across the dry plain, its legs pounding hard.

Rhinos can run fast for short distances. They reach speeds up to 30 miles per hour. That is faster than most people can run!

Rhinos have large, heavy bodies. Their thick skin and strong muscles help them move quickly when needed.

Rhinos get tired after just a few minutes of running. These short bursts help them escape danger or charge at threats.

A rhino's legs are short but very strong. Each foot has three toes with tough nails.

MUD BATHS

Splash! A rhino rolls in thick mud. It looks so happy!

Rhinos love to take mud baths. They roll and wallow in wet, sticky mud. The mud covers their whole body.

Mud helps rhinos stay cool. This thick layer also works like sunscreen. It protects their skin from the hot sun.

The dried mud keeps bugs away too. Flies and ticks cannot bite through it. Rhinos may spend hours in their favorite mud holes.

Oxpecker birds often sit on rhinos at mud wallows. These birds eat the ticks and bugs that the mud missed!

CRASH
COURSE

Grunt! Two rhinos stand near each other. They sniff the air.

A group of rhinos is called a **crash**. But most rhinos live alone. They like their own space.

Female rhinos sometimes stay together. Mothers and calves form small groups. These family groups help protect the babies.

Male rhinos usually live by themselves. They mark their **territory** with dung piles. These smelly piles tell other rhinos to stay away.

White rhinos are more social than black rhinos. They may gather in groups of up to fourteen.

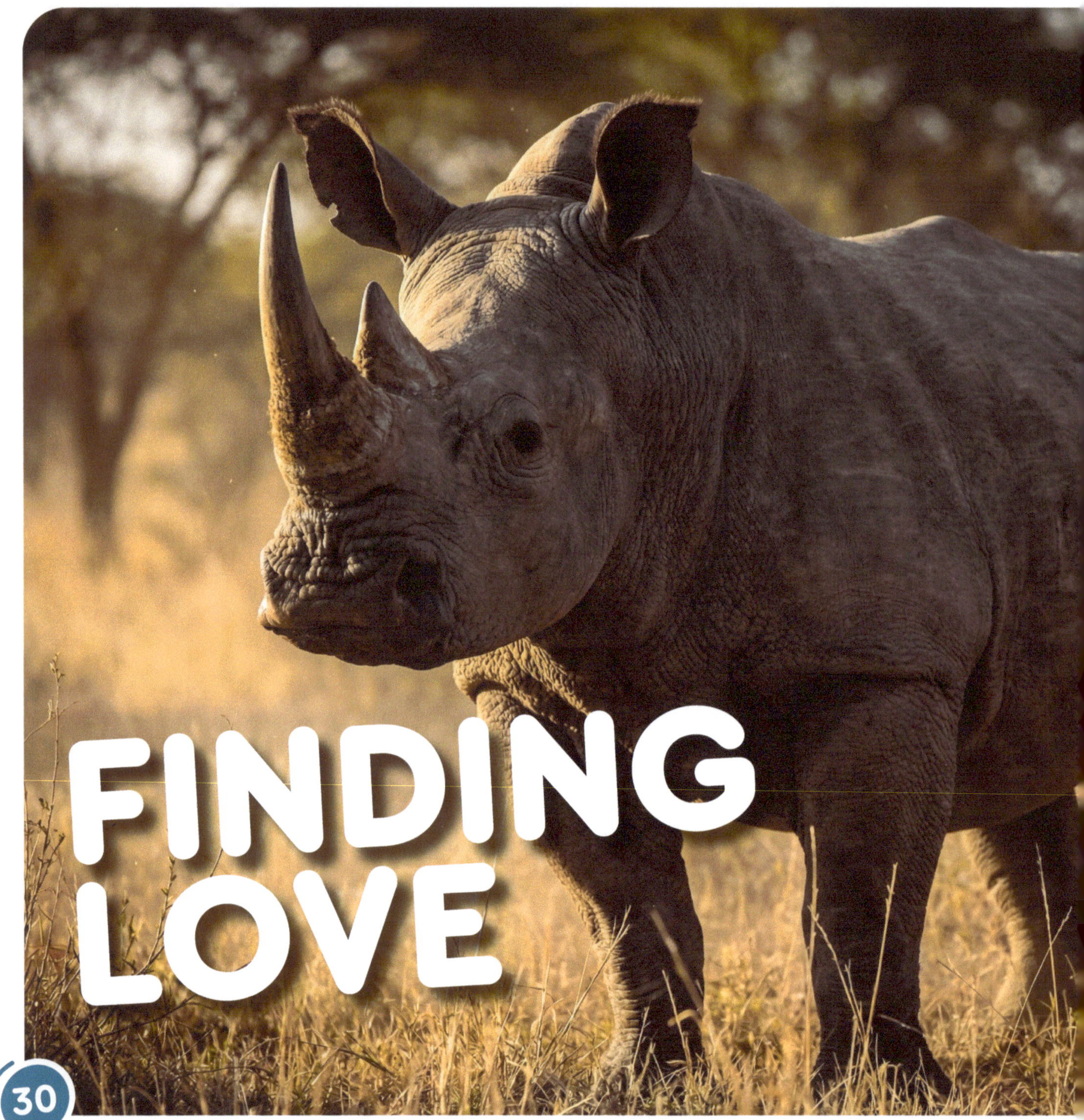

FINDING
LOVE

Snap! A male rhino lifts his head. He smells a female nearby.

Rhinos can mate at any time of year. Males and females find each other by smell. They follow scent trails left in dung and urine.

Males also make loud sounds. They whistle and grunt to get attention.

Once they mate, the male leaves. The female will then be pregnant for about 16 months. That is longer than most animals on Earth!

Female rhinos usually have one calf every two to five years. Twins are very rare.

CUTE CALVES

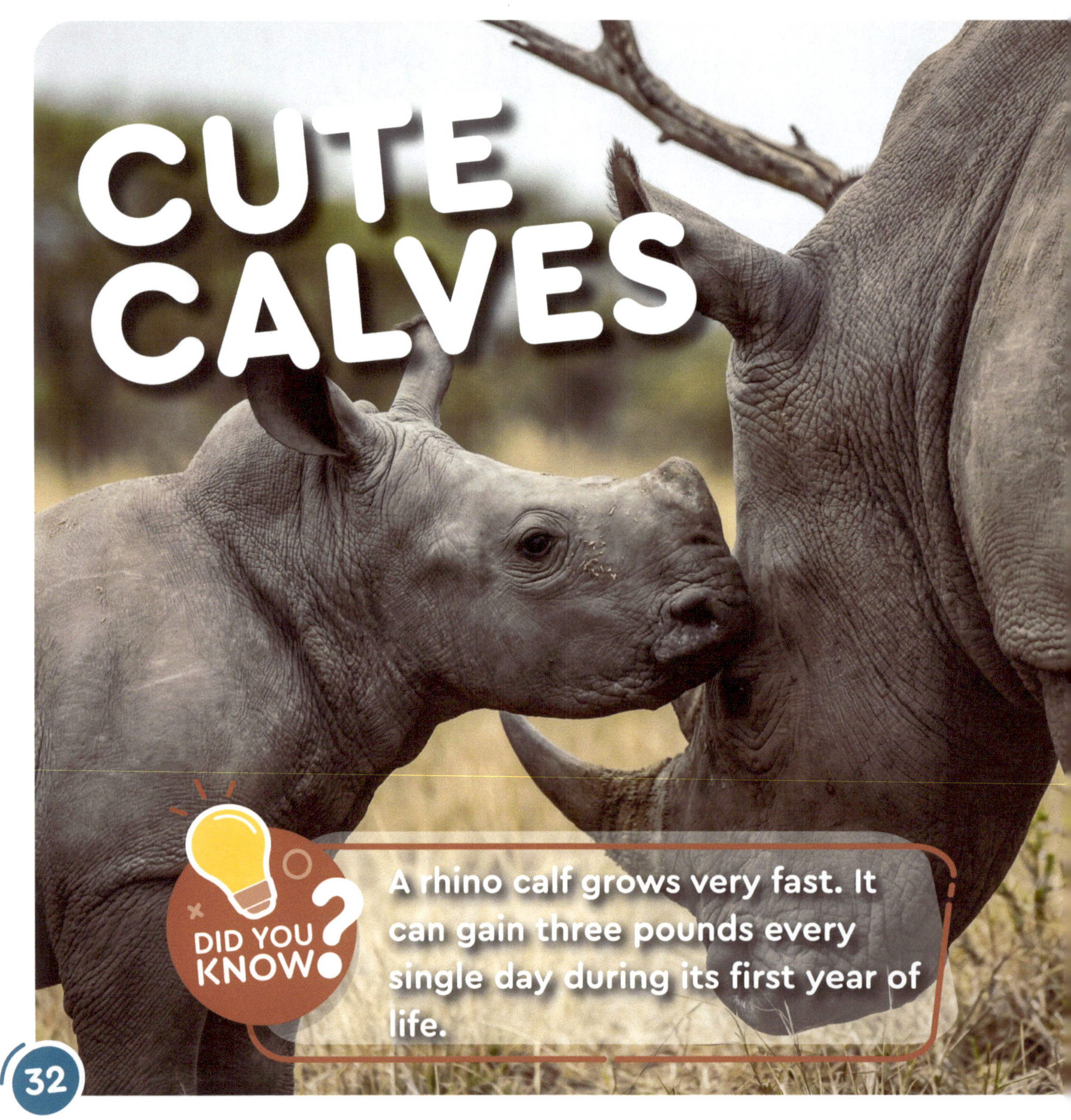

DID YOU KNOW?

A rhino calf grows very fast. It can gain three pounds every single day during its first year of life.

Squeak! A baby rhino stays very close to its mother.

Baby rhinos are called calves. A newborn calf weighs about 100 pounds. That is already the size of most 7th graders!

Calves can stand and start walking within one hour of birth. Even so, a calf stays close to its mother most of the time.

Mother rhinos feed their calves milk for about 18 months. Young rhinos also start eating plants after a few months.

Calves stay with their mothers for two to three years. Then they go off on their own.

MIGHTY
MOMS

A mother rhino stands guard. Her calf hides behind her.

Mother rhinos are very protective. They keep their calves safe from danger. A mother will charge at any threat.

Mothers also teach their calves important skills. Young rhinos learn where to find water. They learn which plants are good to eat.

Mother rhinos and calves use special sounds to find each other. This helps mom stay close day and night. If danger comes, she puts her body between the threat and her baby.

DID YOU KNOW?

Calves stick close to their mother until they are about three years old.

HORN
HUNTERS

Click! A camera trap takes a photo. Rangers use these to watch for poachers.

Rhinos face a big problem. Some people hunt them for their horns. This is against the law. It is called **poaching**.

Some people believe the horns have magical healing powers. They want the horns for medicine.

Poaching has made rhinos very rare. Some rhinos have fewer than 100 left in the wild.

Rhino horn is worth more than gold! But it's not magical and doesn't work as medicine.

RESCUE RANGERS

Roar! A helicopter flies low over grassland. Rangers spot rhinos below.

People around the world work to save rhinos. Rangers guard them day and night. They patrol large areas on foot and in trucks.

Some rhinos wear tracking devices. Scientists use these to follow their movements. This helps keep the animals safe from danger.

Zoos also help rhinos survive. They raise baby rhinos and teach people about these amazing animals.

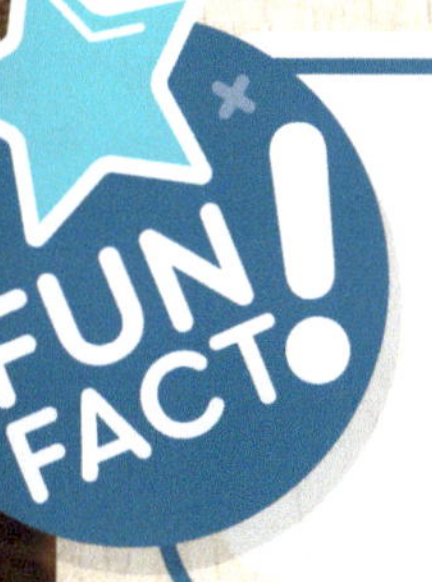

Some rhino reserves use drones to watch over animals and spot poachers from the sky.

GLOSSARY

keratin
The hard material that makes up rhino horns, your fingernails, and your hair.

herbivores
Animals that only eat plants and never eat meat.

territory
An area of land that an animal lives in and protects as its own.

crash
a group of rhinos

poaching
Hunting animals when it is against the law.

* 9 7 9 8 8 9 8 1 8 1 1 8 5 *